Scariest Places
on
Earth

DEATH VALLEY

By Grace Vail

Gareth Stevens
PUBLISHING

Please visit our website, www.garethstevens.com. For a free color catalog of all our high-quality books, call toll free 1-800-542-2595 or fax 1-877-542-2596.

Library of Congress Cataloging-in-Publication Data

Vail, Grace.
Death Valley / by Grace Vail.
    p. cm. — (Scariest places on Earth)
Includes index.
ISBN 978-1-4824-1147-8 (pbk.)
ISBN 978-1-4824-1148-5 (6-pack)
ISBN 978-1-4824-1146-1 (library binding)
1. Death Valley (Calif. and Nev.) — Juvenile literature. 2. Death Valley National Park (Calif. and Nev.) — Juvenile literature. I. Vail, Grace. II. Title.
F868.D2 V25 2015
979.4—d23

First Edition

Published in 2015 by
Gareth Stevens Publishing
111 East 14th Street, Suite 349
New York, NY 10003

Copyright © 2015 Gareth Stevens Publishing

Designer: Katelyn E. Reynolds
Editor: Therese Shea

Photo credits: Cover, p. 1 Kunal Mehra/Flickr Open/Getty Images; cover, pp. 1–24 (background texture) Eky Studio/Shutterstock.com; cover, pp. 1–24 (creepy design elements) Dmitry Natashin/Shutterstock.com; p. 5 (image) sprokop/iStock/Thinkstock.com; p. 5 (map) Uwe Dedering/Wikipedia.com; p. 7 Ralph Crane/Time & Life Pictures/Getty Images; p. 9 Globe Turner, LLC/Getty Images; p. 10 Eric Isselée/iStock/Thinkstock.com; p. 11 (roadrunner) peterjquinn/iStock/Thinkstock.com; p. 11 (desert bighorn) James Phelps/iStock/Thinkstock.com; p. 11 (bobcat) Fuse/Thinkstock.com; p. 11 (kangaroo rat) Design Pics/Thinkstock.com; p. 13 Robyn Beck/AFP/Getty Images; p. 15 adibilio/iStock/Thinkstock.com; p. 17 Dennis Flaherty/Photo Researchers/Getty Images; p. 19 Pete Ryan/National Geographic/Getty Images; p. 21 Buena Vista Images/Stone/Getty Images.

Printed in the United States of America

CPSIA compliance information: Batch #CS15GS: For further information contact Gareth Stevens, New York, New York at 1-800-542-2595.

CONTENTS

Words in the glossary appear in **bold** type the first time they are used in the text.

LOWEST, HOTTEST, DRIEST

Most people don't visit Death Valley in the southwestern United States expecting to find grassy fields and comfortable temperatures. They think the opposite: a sandy desert with hot temperatures. Although parts of Death Valley are like this, visitors may also see fields of wildflowers, shallow lakes, and towering mountains.

Death Valley is a place of **extremes**. It's the hottest and driest place in North America. It's also at the lowest **elevation**. Read on to learn more about Death Valley and to find out why it has such a scary name!

4

Nevada

California

Death Valley is located mostly in southeastern California, but a small area reaches into Nevada.

"GOODBYE, DEATH VALLEY"

In the winter of 1849, a group of travelers headed west to California in search of gold. They were given a map that showed a shortcut to the gold fields through a valley. Eager for riches, a few people decided to follow the shortcut rather than the safer path. It was a decision that nearly killed them all.

They wandered for weeks and nearly starved to death in the valley. As the travelers climbed through the mountains, one of them turned and said, "Goodbye, Death Valley." The name stuck.

Four people in the group that traveled through Death Valley during the winter of 1849–1850 died before they could get out. This photo shows people re-creating the journey.

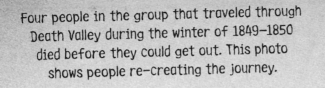

SURROUNDED

Death Valley is large enough for people to get lost in, especially if they're on foot or traveling by wagon. It's about 140 miles (225 km) long and 5 to 15 miles (8 to 24 km) wide.

To the west are the Panamint Mountains, through which the settlers who named Death Valley had to go to reach the California gold fields. There are mountains to the east as well, including the Black, the Grapevine, and the spooky-sounding Funeral Mountains.

The Black, the Grapevine, and the Funeral Mountains are all part of the Amargosa mountain range.

FRIGHTENING OR FUN?

The floor of Death Valley is sinking very, very slowly! The lowest point of all is called Badwater **Basin**. It's 282 feet (86 m) below sea level.

LAST CHANCE RANGE

INYO MOUNTAINS

DEATH VALLEY NATIONAL PARK

GRAPEVINE MTS.

DEATH VALLEY

FUNERAL MTS.

Amargosa

NEVADA
CALIFORNIA

N

ASH MEADOWS N.W.R.

Owens Lake

PANAMINT

Haiwee Res.

Badwater Basin
(Lowest Point in
U.S., -282 ft.)

RANGE

BLACK MTS.

GREENWATER RANGE

0   10   20 mi
0   10   20   30 km

ADAPTED TO DEATH VALLEY

Death Valley animals have **adapted** to living in harsh conditions. Many animals are nocturnal. That means they're mostly active at night, so they can avoid the hot sun. Desert bighorn sheep move higher up in the mountains when it gets too hot. Roadrunners, rabbits, kangaroo rats, coyotes, and bobcats also call Death Valley home.

Wild **burros** can be found in Death Valley as well. They're related to burros lost or left behind by **miners** and travelers more than 100 years ago!

roadrunner

desert bighorn
sheep

bobcat

kangaroo rat

Besides these animals, more than 300 **species** of birds and
35 species of **reptiles** can be found in Death Valley, too.

DEVILS HOLE PUPFISH

Death Valley often gets less than 2 inches (5 cm) of rain a year. However, even fish have found a way to live there!

Devils Hole is a pool in a deep **cavern** in Nevada. Devils Hole pupfish are less than 1 inch (2.5 cm) long. They can live in waters as warm as 93°F (34°C). However, they're dying out. Just 35 were seen in 2013. That's the fewest ever counted.

Pupfish are also found in other places in Death Valley. These fish, too, are in danger of dying out.

FRIGHTENING OR FUN?

To count the Devils Hole pupfish, cave divers have to climb down about 100 feet (30 m). Would you climb into a place called Devils Hole?

Scientists aren't sure why Devils Hole pupfish are disappearing. They tried raising some away from Devils Hole, but the fish soon died.

ROOTED IN DEATH VALLEY

Death Valley is very, very hot about 5 months of the year. The rest of the year is still pretty warm, though! Death Valley doesn't receive much rain because of the surrounding mountains. However, when it does rain, wildflowers may quickly pop up!

Death Valley is home to more than 1,000 kinds of plants. About 50 species can only be found in the special conditions there. These plants often have roots that grow very deep or spread wide in search of water.

Some Death Valley plants have roots that reach down more than 10 times the height of an adult person!

Visitors to Death Valley can see many kinds of **succulents,** including cacti like this flowering one.

15

MOVING ROCKS?

There's a mystery on Death Valley's Racetrack **Playa** (PLY-uh). Heavy rocks have been found with long trails behind them. That means they're moving. However, no one has ever seen them in motion! There are no tracks near the rocks to show that people or animals were doing it. So what's happening?

Some people think that the tracks are made when the playa turns to mud after a rain or is covered by ice in winter. They believe the rocks are set in motion by wind, and they slide across Racetrack Playa.

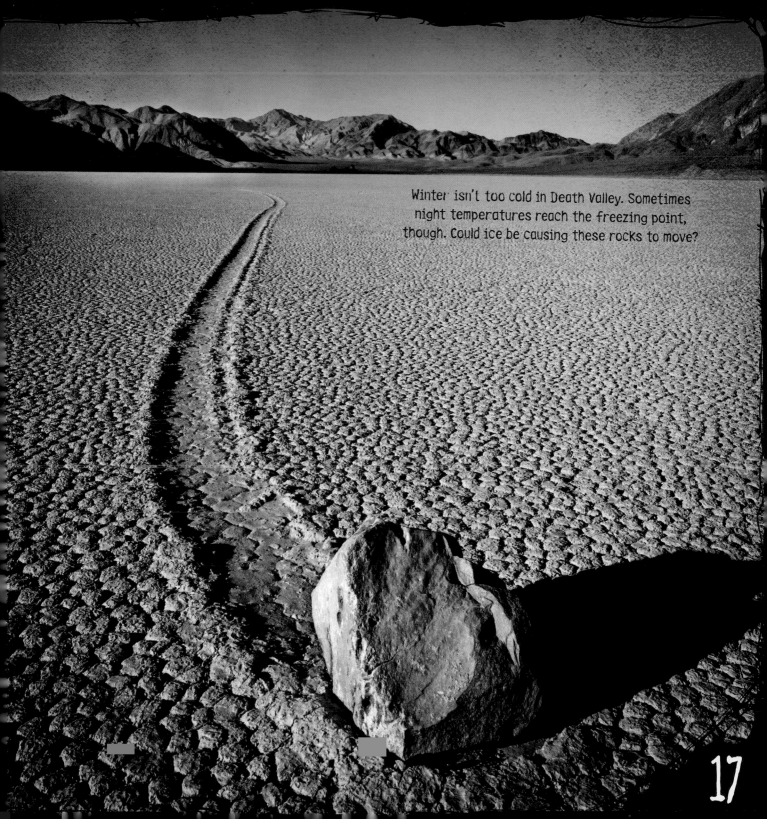

Winter isn't too cold in Death Valley. Sometimes night temperatures reach the freezing point, though. Could ice be causing these rocks to move?

17

GHOST TOWNS!

Ghost towns are towns with few or no people that were once very busy and crowded. Death Valley ghost towns were built by people working in nearby gold, copper, and silver mines in the late 1800s and early 1900s. However, when the mines were used up, people **abandoned** the towns.

Skidoo was one of these towns. Founded in 1906 when travelers struck gold, a town of 700 people sprang up. Skidoo was also the site of the only hanging ever in Death Valley! That's pretty scary!

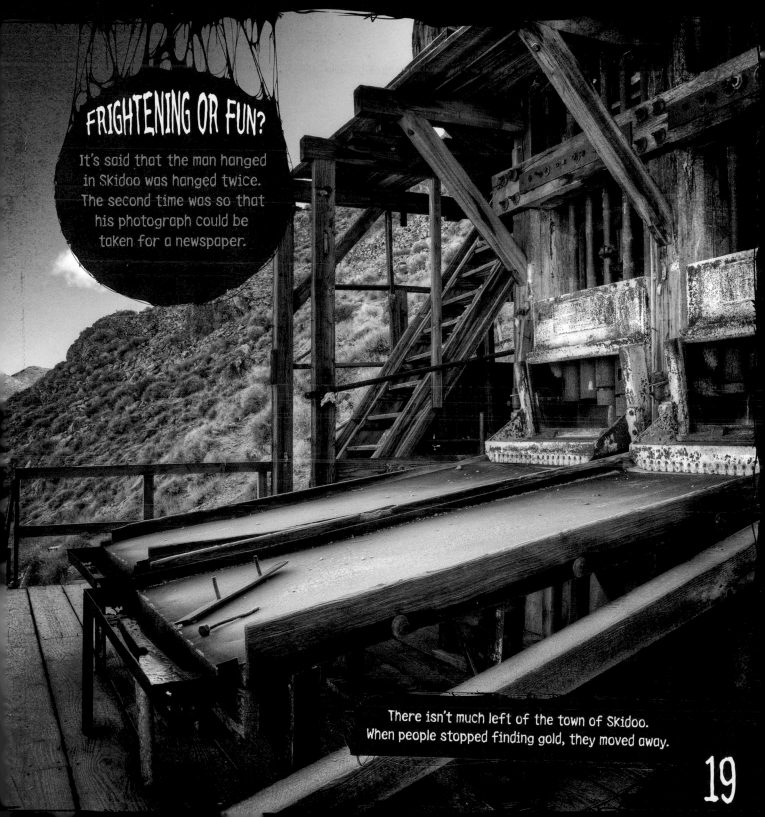

FRIGHTENING OR FUN?

It's said that the man hanged in Skidoo was hanged twice. The second time was so that his photograph could be taken for a newspaper.

There isn't much left of the town of Skidoo. When people stopped finding gold, they moved away.

19

VISIT THE VALLEY

Death Valley deserves its scary name. Even plants and animals adapted to the heat sometimes die from lack of food and water. People have to be very careful when visiting this area. Hikers have gotten lost and become sick from lack of water. Some people have disappeared forever!

Still, people keep coming back to see Death Valley. It's a **unique** part of the United States and the world. It's considered to be so special that it's now a national park.

DEATH VALLEY WEATHER RECORDS

hottest air temperature: 134°F (57°C)

hottest ground temperature: 201°F (94°C)

lowest temperature: 15°F (−9°C)

driest period: 0.64 inch (1.63 cm) of rain from 1931 to 1934

GLOSSARY

abandon: to leave empty or uncared for

adapt: to change to suit conditions

basin: a dip in Earth's surface, somewhat shaped like a bowl

burro: a small donkey

cavern: a large underground cave

elevation: height above sea level

extreme: great or severe

miner: one who takes rocks and other matter from a pit or tunnel

playa: an area of flat, dried-up land

reptile: an animal covered with scales or plates that breathes air, has a backbone, and lays eggs, such as a turtle, snake, lizard, or crocodile

species: a group of plants or animals that are all the same kind

succulent: a plant with thick leaves and stems that can store water

unique: one of a kind

FOR MORE INFORMATION

Books

Dell, Pamela. *Surviving Death Valley: Desert Adaptation*. Mankato, MN: Capstone Press, 2008.

Hamilton, John. *Death Valley National Park*. Edina, MN: ABDO Publishing, 2009.

Pancella, Peggy. *Death Valley National Park*. Chicago, IL: Heinemann Library, 2006.

Websites

Death Valley: 100 Years as Earth's Hottest Spot
www.livescience.com/38054-why-death-valley-hot.html
Discover why Death Valley is so hot.

Death Valley National Park
www.nationalparks.org/explore-parks/death-valley-national-park
Read more about this amazing place and what you can expect when you visit.

Life in Death Valley
www.pbs.org/wnet/nature/deathvalley/
Find out more about Death Valley on a website for the PBS show *Nature*.

INDEX